GOSPEL
LIGHT CHURCH
of GOD *in*
CHRIST JESUS
APOSTOLIC INC.

Ministerial Manual

MARIE E. WILLIAMSON

Order this book online at www.trafford.com
or email orders@trafford.com

Most Trafford titles are also available at major online book retailers.

 www.trafford.com

North America & international
toll-free: 844 688 6899 (USA & Canada)
fax: 812 355 4082

Our mission is to efficiently provide the world's finest, most comprehensive book publishing
service, enabling every author to experience success. To find out how to publish your book,
your way, and have it available worldwide, visit us online at www.trafford.com

ISBN: 978-1-6987-1037-2 (sc)
ISBN: 978-1-6987-1038-9 (e)

Print information available on the last page.

Trafford rev. 12/14/2022

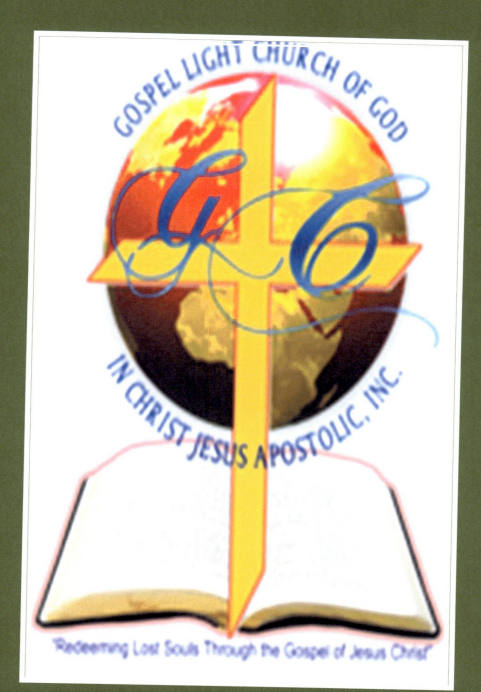

GOSPEL LIGHT CHURCH OF GOD

IN CHRIST JESUS APOSTOLIC, INC.

"Redeeming Lost Souls Through the Gospel of Jesus Christ"

DEDICATION

Gospel Light CHURCH OF GOD IN CHRIST JESUS APOSTOLIC INC. is pleased to present this Minister's Manual to you. May the good Lord bless and encourage you as you use it in fear of God to carry out your ministerial duties.

MINISTERIAL MANUAL

Acts 2:38-39, "Then Peter said unto them, Repent, and be baptized every one of you in the name of Jesus Christ for the remission of sins, and ye shall receive the gift of the Holy Ghost. For the promise is unto you, and to your children and all are afar off, even as many as the Lord our God shall call."

Ephesians 4:11-12

"And he gave some, apostles; and some, prophets; and some, evangelists and some; pastors and some teacher; for the perfecting of the saints, for the work of the ministry, for the edifying of the body of Christ."

Gospel Light Apostolic Ministries Ministerial Manual Committee

Published.

CONTENTS

FOREWORD

The Gospel Light Church of God in Christ Jesus Apostolic Inc. (GLC) aims to benefit our local churches.

The mission of the Gospel Light Church is to spread the Gospel of our Lord and Savior Jesus Christ, to a lost and dying world and to build up the church by carrying out the Great Commission as stated in Matthew 28:19-20. "Go ye therefore and teach all nations, baptizing them in the name of the Father and of the Son and the Holy Ghost: Teaching them to observe all things whatsoever I commanded you: and, lo I am with you always, even unto the end of the world" Amen. "Then Peter said unto them, Repent, and be baptized every one of you in the name of Jesus Christ for the remission of sins, and ye shall receive the gift of the Holy Ghost. For the promise is unto you, and to your children and all are afar off, even as many as the Lord our God shall call" (Acts 2:38). Ministers of the gospel are empowered to preach the gospel, encourage, and support our community with the infallible word of God. To conduct prayer meetings and create a better understanding and love of Christ. The avowal of love to Christ and the gospel and to enlighten and carry on and perpetuate and create a better understanding of the teaching of Christ.

Use it prayerfully, (in fear of God).

Stewart Smith

Bishop

The Gospel Light Church of God in Christ Jesus Apostolic Inc. (GLC)

Newark, New Jersey

MEMBERSHIP COVENANTS OF THE GOSPEL LIGHT CHURCH

I have been baptized in the name of "Jesus Christ" according to Acts 2:38; Acts 10:44 Acts 8:14-17 Acts 19: 1-7 and believe in the baptism of the Holy Ghost with the initial evidence of speaking in tongues as the Spirit gives utterance.

I, therefore, pledge myself by the grace of our Lord Jesus Christ to live up to the covenants of this church.

(1) I will use no tobacco for smoking, chewing, or any of its habitual forms. 11 Cor. 7:1; 1 Cor. 3:16-17 11 Cor 6-18 1 Cor. 6:19-20; Isaiah 55:2

(2) (I will never be intoxicated with wine or by any strong drink. 1 Cor. 6:10 Ephesians 5:18 Prov. 20:1.

(3) (In like manner also, that women adorn themselves in modest apparel which becomes women professing godliness. 1 Timothy 2:9-10 Genesis 35: 1-4.

(4) (I will always abstain from those things that would appear evil to my brethren in the church and the unsaved. 1 Cor.10:28-32, 1 These. 5:22.

(5) (I will never forsake the assembling together of ourselves but will be present at every service, except at times when I find it quite impossible to attend. Heb. 10:25; Matt 18:20.

(6) (I will take no evil report against an Elder or any member of my assembly, but will always seek to prove the things I hear before I accept them. Titus: 3:2; 1 Timothy 5:19-21.

(7) (I will never allow myself to be found thinking or judging by corrupt thoughts of any of God's people but will always think the best of things I cannot understand until I can prove otherwise. Titus 1:15: Phil. 4:8-9.

(8) (I will not take my brother or sister in the Lord before the courts but will always take them to the church in matters where I find it impossible to settle myself. 1Cor. 6:1-6.

(9) (I will have no fellowship with the unfaithful works of Darkness, but I will always reprove the wrong I happen to discover in any member of my assemble; if no amendment, I will take two or three others to help adjust the matter, then, if this fails to bring the desired results. I will take the matter to the church. Eph. 5:11: Matt. 18:15-17

(10) (I will never be yoked with an unbeliever by marrying him or her after I am saved. 11 Cor. 6:14-15.

(11) (As a woman, I will never exercise leadership or usurp authority over an Elder who is spirit-filled in the church 1 Timothy 2: 11-12.

(12) (Upon the first day of the week, I will always pay Tithes and Offerings of money and other things as God had prospered me during the week. 1 Cor. 16:2; 11 Cor. 9:6-8.

(13) (I will always report to the church whenever, I am sick, and report sickness of other members whenever I know of them. James 1:22: James 5:14-15.

(14) (I will always share with the other saints a part of the financial or other obligation of my assembly whenever I am called upon to do so.11 Cor. 8:13-14; 11 Cor.9:7.1

(15) (I will always give due respect to those who are above me in the Lord whatever may be their office in the church. Heb. 13:17.

(16) (I will never rebuke an Elder but will admonish him as a father. 1 Timothy 5:1.

(17) (1 Cor. 11 Above covering the head in worship 1 Cor.11 1-5 & 7 Every man praying or prophesying having his head covered, dishonoureth his head. But every woman that prayeth or prophesieth with her head uncovered dishonoureth her head.

General Apostolic Affirmation of Faith

What we believe: Statement of Faith

Authority of the Word

"Knowing this that no prophecy of the scripture is of any private interpretation. For the prophecy came not in old time by the will of man: but holy men spake as they were moved by the Holy Ghost" (2 Peter 1:20-21).

Salvation – The New Birth

We believe that no one can enter the kingdom of God unless being born again. The New Birth (being born again) includes genuine repentance, water baptism in the name of the Lord Jesus Christ, and the baptism of the Holy Ghost, evidenced of speaking with other tongues as the Spirit gives utterance (John 3:3-7, Acts 2:38, Titus 3:5, James 1:18).

Baptism of the Holy Ghost

We believe that the outpouring of the Spirit on the day of Pentecost marked a new era in the Spirit dealing with mankind as prophesied by Joel (Joel 2:28-29 and Isaiah 28:11); the Holy Ghost being the gift to every believer in this age of grace. We believe that speaking with tongues as the Spirit gives utterance (Acts 2:4) is the initial evidence of the indwelling of the Spirit; not only on the day of Pentecost for the one hundred and twenty initial believers but for all believers for all times.

The Lord's Supper

The Lord's Supper is a memorial service instituted by the Lord Jesus Christ. It is to be commemorated by believers only and is done in remembrance of the Lord Jesus' death, burial, and resurrection. The unleavened bread and the fruit of the vine are symbolic of his flesh and blood (1 Corinthians 11:24-26, St. Luke 11:15-20, St John 13:1-17).

The Second Coming of Jesus Christ

We believe in the personal and imminent return of our Lord Jesus Christ to rapture the Church (1Thessalonians 4:16-17, Matthew 24: 30-42, Revelation 1:7, Acts 1:11, Matthew 24:31-46).

We believe that there is only One God (**Monotheism**). We believe that Jesus was both human and divine: creator and creature; God manifested in the flesh, the only person of the Godhead, the eternal Father made visibly; apart from whom there is no God (Matthew 1:21, John 5:43). We also believe that in Jesus dwelleth all the fullness of the Godhead bodily, for it pleased the Father that in Him should all the fullness dwell. (Colossians 1:19, Colossians 2:9).

We believe in the death, burial, and resurrection of our Lord Jesus Christ. We believe that He ascended into heaven and sent His Holy Spirit (the comforter). *1 Corinthians 15:20, Acts 2:2-4.*

We believe the only way into the kingdom of God is through repentance of sin, water baptism by immersion in the name of Jesus Christ, and affirmation by receiving the gift of the Holy Ghost with the initial evidence of speaking in tongues as the spirit of God gives utterance. *Acts 2:38*.

SECTION 1: CONSTITUTION

Constitution of the Gospel Light Apostolic Ministries Incorporated Operating From 684 Springfield Avenue Newark, New Jersey 07103

CONSTITUTION OF THE GOSPEL LIGHT APOSTOLIC MINISTRIES INCORPORATED

To launch this Ministry on a more effective and sound foundation, we the primary members confirm our trust that God's people should be successfully equipped to preach God's gospel.

ADMISSION TO CHURCH MEMBERSHIP

Only those can be accepted as members of the Gospel Light Church of God in Christ Jesus Apostolic. Who now and who shall continue to subscribe to a belief that the church is one body to be established as a house of prayer and religious worship discipline rules, regulations, rituals rites, ceremonies, and practices? Which now being, or from the time prescribe, designate formulates proclaim, and establish by the governing, body of the Gospel Light Church; and to a declaration that they accept the teachings so the Apostolic Doctrine, and avowal of repentance of their sins. Baptisms in the name of our Lord Jesus Christ according to the practices outlined in Acts 2:38 and receiving the Holy Ghost as in Acts 2:38. Members should have a common belief, we hold that water baptism in Jesus' name for the remission of sins (St. Luke 24:47, Acts 2:38). Water baptism does not remove the old Adamic nature of the individual but takes the curse under which the whole creation lives because of the fall of Adam. Water baptism is the entrance into the church not the perfection of the church (Acts 2:4).

Section 11- <u>How Membership is Obtained</u>

Membership is open to all members of the body of Christ, which is the only true church, the bride of Christ purchased by His blood at Calvary (Ephesians 1:22-23). The applicant assembles represented by its leader, will be required to complete the application process of Section IX.

Page 14

Section 111-Admission

3

Saints that become a member of GLM as well as those that were baptized there are required to register their names and addresses and other vital information to the secretary once given full membership.

1. The pastor is the legal presiding Bishop of the member assemble

Article III – Officers

Section 1-name of Officers

1. A Board of Directors consisting of Presidents, Vice Presidents, Secretaries /Administrators, Treasure, and other Board Members shall govern the Ministry.

2. The duties of the Board are as follows:

    a. To make all legal transactions, which the ministry shall desire concerning all, matters of any importance about the spiritual, moral, and material affairs of the national ministry.

Pastoral Support

1. If a Pastor or leader is ill, incapacitated, leaves their assemble, diseased, or dismiss for misconduct-insubordinate, etc., any of the local assemble that work with Gospel Light Church (GLC) may assist in appointing ministry helps as needed or help in recommending a pastor to take charge. This kind of intervention will only be upon written request by the governing body of that assembly.

2. **Transfer of Membership**

3. Understandably, members will move between ministries, for a variety of reasons, so this must be handled appropriately. Careful thought must be given to the process to reduce

conflicts between leaders and ensure the crucial responsibility of saving souls. GLC will act as an independent mediator while observing the following guidelines.

-) **Marriage**

  The pastors must have a say in the matter at the earliest phase of the procedure.

  As servants of God pastors must use wise and unselfish judgments, especially when it requires that the husband take up membership at the wife's home church.

Leaders must realize that people have a right to make choices.

b. Relocation

Members should secure a letter of recommendation from their previous church and present it to the new pastor.

c. Mistrust

  i. Honesty, confidentially, and good character must be upheld in reserve by leaders as this builds respect from its members for the leadership

d. **Disciplinary situations**

  i. Pastors need to talk with each other about disciplinary actions.

  ii. A member of another assembly who visits another assembly three or more consecutive Sundays should speak to the host Pastor.

  iii. In such a caste if a transfer is requested or sufficient reason is disclosed that indicates the presence of serious issues the pastor should tell the person that attempts will be made to contact the previous pastor.

iv. The pastor should try his endeavor best to resolve the situation.

v. It is important in all transfers made that pastors make every attempt to talk with each other to avoid impairment or severance of relationships.

Financial Assistance

The Gospel Light Church Ministries is not a lending institution. Nonetheless, if any member is in need financially and asked for the assistance of GLC, the Board will review the request and respond in a timely way.

Members Meeting

1. Members' meetings of Gospel Light Church Ministries are announced a few days before the meeting date.

2. Officers or Board meetings can be called at any time by the Bishop or an appointed Board member.

3. A quorum shall consist of two-thirds of the eligible members.

4. A majority vote of the quorum shall be considered final.

ARTICLE V1-VOTING

1. The Gospel Light Ministries require you to be at least 18 years old to vote in their matters and be in good standing in church service attendance and be faithful to God.

2. One is required to attend at least 6 meetings before the voting date and is 70% associated.

3. One must be a GLM for a year.

4. All voting will be a confidential ballot on a subject about people's reputation, possessions acquisitions, selection of officers, or any subjects deemed by the leadership to be of a nature that could cause dissension.

ARTICLE VII-Tenure of Office

1. The office is held for four (4) years.

2. The office of a suitable member usually serves for two four-year periods (a total of eight (8) consecutive years).

3. Four years is the expected time for members to wait before they are eligible for re-election.

4. The Board reserves the right to assign a temporary replacement until the electoral process can be implemented for a permanent replacement in places where there is a rare situation such as death, resignation, illness, or a breakdown in ethical standings.

ARTICLE VIIII- AMENDMENTS

Only a quorum of members can make changes to this constitution.

ARTICLE IX – ORDINATION GUIDELINES AND REQUIREMENTS

POLICY AND PROCEDURE

1. **Purpose**

   a. To set guidelines for Gospel Light Apostolic Ministries ordinations.

   b. To describe which office will be managed through GLM.

   c. To designate the scope of GLM's jurisdiction.

d. To advance and publish essential rules of criteria for national and local appointments.

2. **Scope**

a. GLM to be the vehicle through which ordination of the office of Bishops only is done at the Annual GLM Conferences.

b. The only ones eligible for ordination at the GLM Conferences are clergy members.

c. GLM shall participate and support where needed or requested, in other ordination and appointments done at the local assemblies.

3. **Requirement**

a. Education

• Applicants should submit a certificate from a Bible College in Ministerial Studies or effectively complete an approved evaluation. Candidates must also be fluent in the language of their choice.

b. Character

• One must serve for at least 10 years under one leadership. However, transfers candidate will be nominated based on the reason for relocation

• Applicants must be known for their ministerial services and faithfulness.

• Must also meet Biblical requirements. 1 Timothy 3:1-12, Titus 1:5-9, Titus 2:1-8.

4. **Guidelines**

a. The office of a Bishop requires the following to be given to GLM BOD for approval:

- A letter of intent from the local church.

- A letter of reference from the local church.

- Three letters of recommendation from respectable Clergy (names and addresses to be submitted to sources the letters).

- Two-letter of references from community officials.

- Two letters of recommendation from family members.

- Present police records or reasonable explanations.

- All reference must pertain length of time known and of the relationship.

b. For all other offices of ordination by the local church, the following is required to be submitted for the approval of the BOD and furthered to the GLM BOD for approval (as required by GLM)

- A letter of reference from the local church.

- Two letters of recommendation from respectable Clergy.

- Two-letter of references from community officials.

- Present police records or reasonable explanations.

5. **Approval**

a. Information received will be revised by GLM or a committee approved for that position.

b. A once approved applicant will be informed, and preparation made for the next step in the process.

c. If denied the candidate will be notified after all references submitted are checked.

List of Requirements for all Offices –Tim 3: 1-12

• Self-control- 1 Timothy 3: Tit 1:8

• Hospitable - 1 Timothy 3:2 Tit 8

• Able to teach

• Not violent bit gentle

• Not quarrelsome

• Not a lover of money

• Not a recent convert

• Has a good reputation with outsiders

• Not overbearing

• Not quick-tempered

• Loves what is good

• Upright, holy

• Discipline

- Above reproach (blameless).

- Husband of one wife.

- Not given to wine

- Having his children in subjection with all importance.

- Patient

Additional for Deacons

- Not double-tongued

- Sober

- Not greedy for filthy lucre

- Not slanderers

- Faithful in all things

- Husband of one wife

- Rule their children and household well.

- Must also first be grave.

SECTION 2 CHURCH ADMINISTRATION PROCEDURES

Suggested Program for Weekly Sunday Morning Worship Service

Sunday morning service is the most important fellowship for the local community, where Christians and the unsaved join together in one assembly to surrender their lives to God. While born-again Christians worship God because they have a personal relationship with Him. The unsaved persons come to experience the power of the Holy Ghost therefore the service is properly tailored to invoke the presence of God and be spirit-led, so all can experience the Glory of God.

Consecration Prayer

Choir Processional

Invocation

Scripture Reading

Praise & Worship

Announcement

Offering

Choir Rendition

Sermon

Alter Call

Benediction

THE MATRIMONIAL SERVICES – WEDDINGS

Weddings are very special occasions. Whether there are two witnesses or many others, weddings are filled with love, joy, and tranquility. The union of one man and one woman is reminiscent of the relationship shared between Christ and the Church. The minister must therefore conduct this sacred and love-filled occasion with utmost order and respect.

WEDDING

Format 1

Minister:

Dearly beloved, we are gathered together here in the sight of God and in the presence of this company, to join together this man and this woman in holy matrimony.

Marriage is an honorable estate, instituted by God, blessed by our Lord Jesus Christ, and declared by Saint Paul to be honorable among men. It is therefore not to be entered into unadvisedly or lightly, but reverently, soberly, advisedly, and in the fear of God.

Let us, therefore under this sacred act, invoke the divine presence of God upon this occasion so that you both may be truly and eternally joined together by the Holy Spirit.

Now here are the words of the Holy Scripture concerning those who fear the Lord as recorded in

Psalms:128

"Blessed is every one that fears the Lord; that walketh in his ways. For thou shalt eat the labor of thin hands, it shall be well with thee. Thy wife shall be a fruitful vine by the side of thine house thy children like olive plants around thy table. Yea, thou shall see the children's children."

If any man can show any just cause why this man and this woman should not be lawfully joined together, let him now speak, or else hereafter hold his peace.

Ministerial Charge

Minister:

I require and charge you both, as you will stand in the Dreadful Day of judgment, that if either of you knows of any impediment as to why you may not be joined together in holy matrimony, that ye do now confess it. For be well assured, that if any person is joined in holy matrimony, other than as God's Word doth allowed, the marriage is not lawful.

Minister:

[Name of groom], please repeat the following declaration

I, {name of groom},

…do solemnly declare,

…that I know not of any lawful impediment

…why I may not be join in holy matrimony

…to {name of bride}

Minister:

[Name of bride], please repeat the following declaration,

I, [name of bride],

…do solemnly declare,

…that I know not of any lawful impediment

…why I may not be joined in holy matrimony

…to [name of groom].

The Sacred Vows

Minister:

Since it is your delight to join in this sacred matrimony, pause for a moment, and look around. Your loves ones and friends are assembled here today to rejoice with you, to show their wish for your happiness.

I now charge you both, as you stand in the presence of Almighty God and His holy angels, to remember that true love and commitment to your marriage vows are required. Be true to the solemn vows you are about to take, with tender consideration for each other! Conduct your lives in sincerity and truth!

Minister:

[name of groom], do you take this woman to be your wedded wife, and do you solemnly promise, before God and witnesses, that you will love her, comfort her, honor and keep her, in sickness and in health, and that, forsaking all others for her alone, you will perform unto her all the duties that a husband owes to his wife, until God, by death shall separate you?

Groom: I do

Minister:

[name of bride],

Do you take this man to be your wedded husband, and do you solemnly promise, before God and witnesses, that you will love him, comfort him, honor and keep him, in sickness and in health, and that, forsaking all others for him alone, you will perform unto him all the duties that a wife owes to her husband, until God, by death shall separate you?

Bride: I do

Minister:

Who gives this woman to be married to this man?

Minister:

Since it is your delight to take each other as husband and wife, please join your right hands, and repeat after me, before God and these witnesses the marriage vows.

Minister:

Please repeat after me.

I, [name of groom],

… call upon these persons here present,

… to witness, that I do take thee, [name of groom].

…to be my lawful wedded husband,

…to have and to hold,

…from this day forward,

… for better or for worst,

…for richer, for poorer,

…in sickness and in health

… to love and to cherish,

…therefore [name of groom]

…." Entreat me not to leave thee,

…or to return from following after thee:

…for whither thou goest, I will go

…where thou lodges, I will lodge;

…Thy people shall be my people,

…And my thy God my God,"

… Till death shall separate us,

…according to God's Holy Ordinance,

… and thereto,

…I give thee my faith,

… in the name of Lord Jesus Christ

The Exchange of Rings

Minister: May I have the rings, please?

Minister to the bride:

Will you receive this ring from [name of groom] as a token of his affection, sincerity, and fidelity towards you, and will you wear it as a symbol of your affection, sincerity, and fidelity towards him?

Bride: I will

Minister to the groom:

Minister to the bride:

Will you receive this ring from [name of bride] as a token of his affection, sincerity, and fidelity towards you, and will you wear it as a symbol of your affection, sincerity, and fidelity towards her?

Prayer for the Rings

Heavenly Father, Creator, and sustainer of all humankind, Giver of all spiritual grace, the Author of eternal life, send by the blessing upon thy servants, this man, and woman, who we bless in thy name. Help them to perform and keep their vows and the sacred vow between them made, whereof these rings are given and perceived as a token, and pledge and ever remain in perfect love and peace together and live according to thy through Jesus Christ our Lord. Amen

Minister to the groom:

Please declare the following words as you place the rings on her hand.

With this ring,

… I, thee, wed,

…in the name of the Lord Jesus.

Minister to the Bride:

Please declare the following words as you place the rings on his hand:

…With this ring,

…in the name of the Lord Jesus.

Instruct the Bride and groom to kneel for the prayer

The groom said," He that findeth a wife, findeth a good thing. And obtaineth favor of the Lord"

Declaration of Marriage

Minister:

For as much as [name of groom], and [name of bride], have consented together in holy wedlock and have witnessed the same before God and his company, and thereto have given and pledged their faith, to each other, and have declared the same by joining their right hands and by giving and receiving (a) rings (s). I declared, by the authority committed unto me as a minister of the Gospel of Jesus Christ, and by the authority invested in me by the government of [province/territory] that they are husband and wife, in the Name of the Lord Jesus Christ. Those whom God hath joined together let no man separate.

The groom may now kiss the bride

The blessing (Pronounced by the officiating Clergy)

According to Deuteronomy chapter 28, all these blessings

Will come on you and overtake you if you will hearken unto the voice of the Lord your God:

Blessed shalt thou be in the field,

Blessed shall be thy basket and thy store,

Blessed shalt thou be when thou comest in, and blessed shalt thou be when thou goes out.

He shall cause thy enemies that rise against thee to be smitten before thy face: they shall come out against thee one way and shall flee before thee seven ways.

The Lord shall command the blessing upon thee in thy storehouse, and in all that thou settest thine hand unto,

And all people shall see that thou art called by the name of the Lord, and they shall be afraid of thee.

The signing of the Register

Minister:

Guests will be entertained by a Soloist etc.

Commending Bride and Groom to Witness

Minister:

With pleasure, I now present to you Mr. and Mrs. [surname of groom].

FORMAT 2

Minister:

Dearly beloved, we are gathered together here in the sight of God and in the face of this company, to join this man and this woman together in holy matrimony. As marriage is a sacred institution, it should not be entered into unadvisedly, or lightly, but reverently and in the fear of God. Into this holy estate, the two-person present comes now to be joined. If anyone can show just cause why he or she may not lawfully be joined together, let him speak, or else hereafter hold his peace.

Minister to the Bride and Groom:

I require and charge you two, as ye will answer at the dreadful Day of judgment, when the secret of all hearts shall be revealed, that if either of you knows any impediment why ye may not be lawfully joined together in matrimony, ye do now own up to it. But be well assured, that if any persons are joined together otherwise than as God's Word commanded, their marriage is not lawful.

Minister to the Groom:

[Name of Groom], wilt thou have this woman to be thy wedded wife, to live together after God's laws, in the Holy estate of matrimony? Wilt thou love her, comfort her, honor and keep her, in sickness and in health, and forsaking all others, keep thee only unto her, so long as ye both shall live?

Groom: I will

Minister to the Bride: [Name of Bride], wilt thou have this man to be thy wedded wife, to live together after God's laws, in the Holy estate of matrimony? Wilt thou love her, comfort her, honor and keep her, in sickness and in health, and forsaking all others, keep thee only unto her, so long as ye both shall live?

Bride: I will.

Minister: Who gives this woman to be married to this man?

Giver: I/We do.

Minister: Take the right hand of the bride from the giver and place it in the right hand of the groom. Then address the groom.

[Name of groom], please repeat after me:

I, [name of groom], take thee, [name of bride],

… to be my wedded wife.

…to have and to hold,

…from this day forward,

… for better or for worst,

…for richer, for poorer,

…in sickness and in health

… to love and to cherish,

…till death do us part,

….according to God's holy ordinance;

… and hereto

… I give thee my love (trust).

Minister: Gently have the bride and groom unclasp their hand. Then, have the bride take the groom by his right hands. At this time, address the bride.

Minister to the Bride:

[name of the bride], please repeat after me:

I, [name of bride]… take thee, [name of groom]

… to be my wedded husband,

…to have and to hold,

…from this day forward,

… for better or for worst,

…for richer, for poorer,

…in sickness and in health

… to love and to cherish,

…till death do us part,

….according to God's holy ordinance;

… and hereto

… I give thee my love (trust).

The bride and groom unclasp their hands, at this point the ring (s) is (are) to be presented to the Minister:

Minister to declare the following with the ring (s) in hand:

The marriage rings bear the form of a circle. Void of the point of beginning and end, it is symbolic of eternity. It is made with precious gold, a metal that is least tarnished and most enduring. It, therefore, reflects the permanence and imperishability of the faith which you have both pledged to the other.

Considering that you enter this marriage, which must only be severed by death, it is therefore incumbent upon you to carefully and prayerfully consider the duties, which this honorable undertaking entails. If you diligently carry out your duties, your home, and relationship will overflow with overwhelming happiness, light, love, and blessing from above. If you fail to fulfill your marital obligations, your life will be replete with unhappiness, darkness, and guilt.

The husband must provide for the wife, love her, show her affection and shelter her from harm. Therefore, God commands that a husband love his wife, just as Jesus Christ loves His church and gave his life for her at Calvary.

The Holy Bible instructs a wife to obey her husband. Since Christ is subject to the church, a wife must also be subject to her husband.

Even though you will be people of different sorts, today, you will become one and undivided in interest and reputation, spirit, soul, and, body, to please God, each other, and the community around you.

Prayers for the ring (s)

Minister: Give the bride's ring to the groom. Ask him to place the ring halfway on the finger to the left of the index finger.

Minister to the groom:

Please repeat after me: As a pledge and in token

… of these vows

…With this ring,

… and with all my worldly goods

… I thee endow

…in the name of the Lord Jesus Christ.

Prayer

Our Father, who art in heaven hallowed be thy name thy Kingdom come. Thy will be done on earth as it is in heaven. Give us this day our daily bread, and forgive us our trespasses as we forgive those who trespass against us. And lead us not into temptation, but deliver us from evil, through Jesus our Lord. Amen

Almighty God, Creator, and Savior of all mankind, who gives us life, blesser of all spiritual grace, send thy blessing up these your servants, this man, and this woman, whom we bless in Your Name, that they live in peace and faithfully keep their wedding vows and covenant between them together, and live by thy commandments, through Jesus Christ our Lord. Amen.

Join the hands of the bride and groom, right hand in the right hand.

Minister:

Those whom God hath joined together, let no man put asunder.

(Address the bride and groom, along with the entire Congregation).

For as much as [name of groom], and [name of bride], have consented together in sacred wedlock, and have witnessed the same before God and this gathering of well-wishers, and have given and vow their faith to each other, and have declared their love by giving and receiving of(a) ring (s)and by joining hands, I pronounce that they are husband and wife in the Name of Jesus. Amen

Minister: Instruct the newlyweds to kneel for the prayer of consecration.

Ministerial Prayer

Minister:

Groom may kiss the bride

Singing of the Register

Commending Bride and Groom to Witnesses

MILESTONE ANNIVERSARIES

Minister:

We are assembled here in the presence of God and in the company, to give thanks to God for enabling [name of husband] and [name of wife] to be celebrating_ years of their marriage commitment.

Marriage, as instituted by God, is regulated by His commandments and blessed by our Lord Jesus Christ. We should always remember that God has blessed, sanctified, and established marriage for the welfare and happiness of mankind.

It is indeed gratifying to know that_ years ago, [name of husband], and {name of wife] entered into this mutual esteem and love. To bear with each other's infirmities and weakness, to comfort each other, in sickness, trouble, and sorrow; in honest industry, to each other and their household, in temporal things. To pray and encourage each other in things about God, and to live together as heirs of His grace.

[name of husband] and [name of wife]

Have invited us to share in the celebration of the year of the most sacred relationship, wherein they have covenanted to guard the welfare of each other more carefully than their own. They have affirmed their love before the altar of God; they have pledged their faith one to the other years ago. The life they live is indeed an example for their children and others to follow.

Prayer of Thanksgiving

Minister:

Let us unite in prayer: Most Holy God, who in thy great wisdom has ordained and blessed the institution of marriage, we ask that your richest blessings may be established upon this man and woman, who have solemnly pledged themselves to each other in the bonds of matrimony years ago. Grant that they continue to regard their home to be a holy sanctuary, in which Jesus Christ, our Lord, shall continue to be looked upon us as the head of our family. Until that great and magnificent day, keep them faithful to Thee and each other. Amen.

Minister:

The writer of Hebrews declares that "Marriage is honorable in all and the bed is undefiled: but whoremongers and adulterers God will judge. "Marriage is A God-ordained- institute, intended to meet the needs of a man and a woman and develop them into spiritual maturity. When a man or woman leaves his mother and father and cleaves unto his wife he experiences the oneness of flesh, the union of mind, will, and spirit that comes from the commitment (cleaving) to each other in sacred marriage vows. The fidelity called for by God in a marriage relationship is a human object lesson of the spirit fidelity of Christ and the Church. The Old Testament starts with a marriage in the Garden of Eden. Jesus began His first public ministry by performing His first miracle at the wedding in Cana of Galilee and the Bible ends with the Marriage Supper of the Lamb in New Jerusalem.

The Exchange of Rings

Minister:

Asked for the rings. Make the following statement with the rings in hand: may this beautiful token and pledge symbolize the purity and endlessness of your love.

Minister to the groom:

Please repeat after me:

With this ring,

… I rededicate my life to thee

…in the name of the Lord Jesus Christ.

Minister to the bride:

Please repeat after me:

With this ring,

… I rededicate my life to thee

…in the name of the Lord Jesus Christ.

The Apostle Paul declares that love suffereth long and is kind.

Love envieth not

Love envieth, not itself

Love is not puffed up

Love doth behave itself unseemly

Seeketh not her own

Is not easily provoked

Thinketh no evil

Rejoiced not in iniquity, but rejoice in the truth

Beareth all things

Believeth all things

Hoped all things

Endureth all things

LOVE never falls

Minister: for as much as [name of groom] and [name of bride] have agreed together in sacred wedlock ----- years ago and have witnessed that same before God and others present, I would therefore charge you to continue to be faithful to God in the positions He has placed you both. Continue to be faithful to each other and the Lord Jesus until death.

The Lord bless and keep you both. The Lord causes His face to shine upon you and be gracious to you. The Lord lifts His countenance upon you and grants you peace. In the name of our sinless Master, even Jesus Christ. Amen.

DEDICATION OF CHILDREN

(Christian Parents)

Scripture: 1 Samuel 1:24-28, Mark 10:13-16, Matt19:13-14

The family is a divine institution ordained by God from the beginning of time. Children are a heritage of the Lord committed by Him to their parents, for care, protection, and training for His glory.

By this charge, a parent is expected to follow God's word and instill them in their children. Jesus gave several demonstrations in the Bible of why children should be dedicated unto Him, as shown here in Luke, "And they were bringing even their babies to Him so that He would touch them, but when the disciples saw it, they began rebuking them. However, Jesus called them, saying, "Permit the children to come to me, and do not hinder them, for the kingdom of God belongs to such as these. "Truly I say to you, whoever does not receive the kingdom of God like a child will not enter in at all" (Luke 18, 15-17). Jesus, Himself was an example of how a child should be dedicated as well as in 1 Samuel 1 where Anna spoke these words, "Oh, my Lord! As your soul lives, my Lord, I am the woman who stood here beside you, praying to the LORD. "For this boy, I prayed, and the LORD has given me my petition which I asked of Him. "So, I have also dedicated him to the LORD as long as he lives, he is dedicated to the LORD "And she worshiped the LORD there (1 Samuel 1:26-28).

Charge to the parents

Train up a child in the way he should go, and when he is old, he will not depart from it (Prov.22:6).

These words which I command you this day, shall be upon thy heart; and thou shall teach them diligently unto thy children, and shalt talk to them when thou sittest in thy house, and when thou walkest by the way, and when thou liest down, and when thou risest up (Deut. 6:6-6).

(Optional)

And the Lord said, I know Abraham, that he will command his children and his household after him, and they shall keep the way of the Lord, to do justice and judgment (Gen. 18:19).

These words which I command thee this day shall be upon thy heart; and thou shalt teach them diligently unto the children, and shall talk of them when thou sittest in thy house, and when thou walkest by the way, and when thou liest down, and when thou risest up (Deut, 6:6-7).

Vows

Minister to Parents of a child

1. In the sight of God and the presence of these witnesses do you solemnly ender to bring up this child in the fear and admonition of the Lord?

   Answer: "We Do."

2. Do you promise early to seek to lead this child to accept Jesus as Savior and Lord?

   Answer: "We Do."

3. Do you promise as far as lies to set before this child example of godly and consistent lives?

   Answer: "We Do."

Minster's Address:

This is a happy and significant occasion, which brings us together. Like Mary and Hannah of old, you have brought your child to the House of God today to present him/her to the Lord. You have heard the invitation of the Master: "Suffer the little children to come unto me, and forbid them not, for of such is the Kingdom of heaven."

Dedication of Children (unsaved Parent)

As the parents, godparents, family members, and well-wishers approach the altar to meet the minister, have the choir, or praise and worship singers sing a children's song.

(e.g. "Suffer the Little Children")

Minister:

The family is an important instate ordained by God from the days of old. The word of God said children are the heritage of the Lord to be cared for by loving parents, family, and friends. As parents, it is your God-given responsibility to raise your children in the ways of righteousness, godliness, and exposing your child (ren) to a Godly heritage.

In the presence of the Lord and the company of these witnesses, will you commit to exposing your child (these children) to a Godly heritage and instruction?

Parents: We do

At this point, have a designated reader read Mark 10; 13-16. As the reader reads the final verse, the minister will take the child in his arms. **Mark 10:13-16** As the reader reads the final verse, the minister will take the child in his arms.

- Minster: let us stand as we offer this dear child to the Lord.

- Minister will say a dedicatory prayer,

- Minister: will offer a dedicatory prayer

Since you have presented yourselves before this holy altar of God to dedicate [name of the child(ren)] I charge you to surrender your lives to Jesus Christ. May He favor you with abundant wisdom, knowledge, understanding, and patience for the journey ahead.

MINISTRY OF THE SICK

Introduction

What is our main goal in visiting sick/purpose?

As followers of Christ, we emulate His love and compassion when we show hospitality to all - not only to our Christian family, but even more so to the visitors, our communities, strangers, and those who are less fortunate.

Gospel Light Church's focus on hospitality promotes a strong focus on the needs of others, a willingness to share what we have, and loving hearts seeking sincere relationships with all people by taking special care of our visitors, nurturing new members, and being intentional about fostering an atmosphere of Godly fellowship and love.

Important Information

1. A minister is required to visit the sick.

2. A minister is called to demonstrate Christ-like character while attending to the need of the sick.

3. While visiting the sick a minister should remind the sick of God's undying love for them and that He can heal their condition.

4. A minister should operate in the spirit of imitative, never waiting to be called on to visit.

5. A minister must always be dressed in appropriate attire. Clergy vestments or business casual attire are rather fitting. Avoid casual clothing.

6. A minister should have a small vial of anointing oil and a Bible in hand.

The following outline may be used during a home visit:

Check to ensure that the individual is presentable to receive visitors

1. Upon entrance, greet the ill individual and any other persons present.

2. Engage in meaningful and non-judgmental conversation, asking general questions about the individual's state of being and showing a genuine interest in their life, and if possible, assemble those who are present around the place where the sick person is.

3. Say a brief prayer.

4. Sing a song, if time permits.

5. Read a passage of scripture (Psalm 46, Psalm 91, Psalm 27)

6. Offer a word of encouragement from the passage.

7. Sing another song if possible.

8. Lay hands on the sick person and pray a prayer of intercession on their behalf- do not put pressure on the person's body.

9. Allow the sick to give words of expression.

10. Thank the sick individual for having you.

11. Close with a cooperate benediction.

Please remember that not all setting, such as hospitals permits a long visit of visitors. Also, the person who is sick requires ample time to rest. Therefore, such visitation should be limited to 20-30 minutes.

THE FUNERAL SERVICE

Everyone, as to pass this way in life as the good book, says "It's appointed unto man once to die and after this, the judgment" yet death is a thing no one is prepared for or wants to happen to his or her loved one's or friends. When a death occurs, families, friends, along the surrounding community become overwhelmed by grief, fear, and shock. At this point, the minister of the gospel of Jesus Christ, along with qualified staff, must offer spiritual, emotional, and administrative assistance to the bereaved family.

Immediately after the time of death

Once the minister receives the news of death, it is his/her responsibility to take the initiative to visit the bereaved family within 24 hours of notification, to offer sincere condolences.

The minister should ask the family if they have any particular requests., like the desired location for service, foreign burial, etc, and seek to satisfy them as much as possible. He should also provide the bereaved family with a basic outline for the funeral arrangements.

If asked, the minister should accompany the family to the funeral home and cemetery for the funeral arrangements. (Identity who is in charge of the funeral arrangements). Because the duress of the final arrangements may way a great deal on the bereaved, the minister may have to become the spokesman, as well as comfort and spiritual support to the family. His/her participation in the process also will endure that the procedures of the funeral agreement are in line with the systems and main beliefs of the assembly.

The Final Service

Due to the grief and the sense of loss that the family is experiencing, the minister must handle this service with utmost care.

Most often, the pastor of the congregation will be the one to offer the final sermon for the occasion. There may be cases where the family or pastor him/herself may request or recommend another for the task.

To ensure that this delicate service remains focused and orderly, a moderator should be appointed to oversee and direct the completion of the service.

Order of Service (at funeral home or church)

1. Procession of Clergy, Choir & Bereaved Family

The officiating minister should be at the head of the procession. Promptly, the officiating minister will recite any of the following passages:

"I am the resurrection and the life saith the Lord; he that believeth in me though he were dead, yet shall he live; and whosoever liveth and believed in me shall never die (John 11:25-26).

"I know that my redeemer liveth and He shall stand at the latter day upon the earth: and though after my skin worms destroy this body, yet in my flesh shall I see God! Whom I shall see for myself and mine eyes shall behold, and not another (Job 19:15-27).

We brought nothing into this world, and we can certainly carry nothing out. The Lord gave and the Lord hath taken away. Blessed be the name of the Lord Or Read John 14:1-27

2. **Congregational Song**

    Recommended Song:

    It is Well

    We "ll Understand it Better

    No Not One

    Death Hath No Terrors

    Great is Thy Faithfulness

    Come Unto Faithfulness

    Glory To God

3. **Invocation Prayer**

4. **First Scripture Reading**

    Recommended Scriptures:

    Psalm 27

    Ecclesiastes 3:1-13

    Psalm 40

    Isaiah 14

    Psalm 90

Psalm 139

5. **Ministerial Remarks**

6. **Tributes/ How I knew you**

7. **Choir Selection**

8. **Second Scripture Reading**

   Recommended Scripture:

   Job 14: 1-17

   1 Corinthians 15:35-57

   1 Thessalonians 4:13-18

   Revelation 21

9. **Eulogy**

10. **Congregational Song**

    Recommended Songs:

    When They Ring Those Golden Bells

    How Great Thou Art

    Father Along

    The Solid Rock

There is a Green Hill Far Away

11. **Special Offering (optional) For either the family or for the work of the ministry**

12. **Sermon**

13. **Choir Selection**

14. **Prayer for the family**

15. **Funeral Director Provides Instructions regarding the Internment Congregation**

16. **Recessional**

    Funeral Recession should follow instructions provided by the Funeral directors. Order of exit should begin with funeral directors and casket, followed by the Clergy, followed by the family and family funeral guests.

17. **Recommended Recessional Songs**

    In the Arms of Sweet Deliverance

    When We All Get to Heaven

    To God be the Glory

Once the recessional has arrived at the parking lot, the funeral staff, clergy, family, and well-wishers should head to their designed cars in an orderly fashion. Leaving the church the order of cars should be as follows: (1) funeral coach, (2) clergy car,(3) family car(s), followed by (4) cars of well-wishers.

Interment Services.

After the funeral party has arrived at the cemetery, the minister will lead the pallbearers to the intended place of burial.

As walking at the head of the final processional to the grave site, the Minister shall repeat:

"I am the resurrection and the life, saith the Lord; he that believeth in me, though he were dead, yet shall he live; and whosoever liveth and believeth in me, shall never die.

For we know that if our earthy house of this tabernacle were dissolved, we have a building of God, a house not made with hands, eternal in the heavens.

The minister must position him/herself at the head of the grave.

At that point, while the relatives and well-wishers are assembling around the plot, a series of suitable songs can be sung.

Recommended Hymns/Choruses

Shall We Gather at the River

In the Good Old-Fashioned Way

When the Roll is Called up Yonder

No Grave Can Hold My Body Down

In the Sweet By and By

Goodnight, Goodnight

Meet Me by the River

Till We Meet Again

Final Words for the Departed Christian

Minister:

This service is tailored to mark the final chapter of the life of[deceased name], concluding his/her life from the beginning to the end. Forasmuch, as it pleased the Lord God to call [deceased name] from this world into His eternal rest, we willfully, commit the remains of our dearly beloved servant of the Lord to the ground from which it came. Ashes to ashes, and dust to dust, let us, therefore, be comforted by the great and glorious promise of God's infallible Word, looking for the resurrection of the dead and awesome appearing, whenever a man shall give an answer of the deeds done in his/her body.

For the Departed Unsaved

Minister: This service is tailored to mark the final chapter of the life of[deceased name], concluding his/her life from the beginning to the end. Forasmuch, as it pleased the Lord God to call [deceased name] from this world into His eternal rest, we willfully, commit the remains of our dearly beloved servant of the Lord to the ground from which it came. Ashes to ashes, and dust to dust, let therefore be comforted by the great and glorious promise of God's infallible Word, looking for the resurrection of the dead and awesome appearing, whenever a man shall give and answer of the deeds done in his/her body.

Final Brief Prayer of Consolation

Minister to declare words of benediction upon those assembled

(May the grace of our Lord Jesus be with you all Amen.)

The gathering is waiting for the covering of the casket- a series of songs can be sung. (see list of recommended songs, and choruses above)

Grave Closing

Finally, family friends and cemetery staff may begin to close the grave, as the family asked. Nonetheless, not all families wish to see the lowering of the casket. Some rather leave after the benediction, which leaves the cemetery staff to tend to the closing of the grave.

Entombment or Mausoleum Burials

Use the same ad Graveside Burial, modify where necessary

For Burial Abroad or Elsewhere:

Some families chose to bury their deceased loved ones overseas in their native country. However, because of distance and travel expenses, many are not able to attend these overseas burials. But thank God for the breakthrough in modern technology because we can utilize Zoom, Facebook, and YouTube the following method will be deemed appropriate as it provides a sense of closure for those loved ones and family members who will not be able to travel.

After the funeral service the clergy, choir, pallbearers, and family will leave the sanctuary and head for the parking lot, of the church where the funeral coach is parked.

Once outside the pallbearers, under the direction of the staff from the funeral home, will position the casket in front of the open door of the funeral coach.

It is the minister's responsibility to position him/her at the head of the casket.

Next, while the family and well-wishers are congregated behind the funeral coach, a series of songs may be sung.

Minister:

This service is tailored to mark the final chapter of the life of [deceased name], concluding his/her life from the beginning to the end. Forasmuch, as it pleased the Lord God to call [deceased name] from this world into His eternal rest, we willfully, commit the remains of our dearly beloved servant of the Lord and its final remains in the hands of the Lord as it travels to its final rest. May the peace of God remain and abide with us all until we behold His wonderful face in eternity.

Final Brief Prayer of Consolation

Minister to declare words of benediction upon those assembled

(May the grace of our Lord Jesus be with you all Amen.)

A series of songs can be sung as the pallbearers under the instruction of the funeral home staff, respectfully placing the casket into the coach. The funeral director will now close the coach (see list of recommended songs and choruses above).

The funeral coach will drive off slowly, returning to the funeral home as the faithful continue to sing.

Finally, Minister will greet and console the family and friends, as well as dismiss the people.

MINISTRY OF THE SICK

Introduction

What is our main goal in visiting sick/purpose?

As followers of Christ, we emulate His love and compassion when we show hospitality to all - not only to our Christian family, but even more so to the visitors, our communities, strangers, and those who are less fortunate.

Gospel Light Church's focus on hospitality promotes a strong focus on the needs of others, a willingness to share what we have, and loving hearts seeking sincere relationships with all people by taking special care of our visitors, nurturing new members, and being intentional about fostering an atmosphere of Godly fellowship and love.

Important Information

1. A minister is required to visit the sick.

2. A minister is called to demonstrate Christ-like character while attending to the need of the sick.

3. While visiting the sick a minister should remind the sick of God's undying love for them and that He can heal their condition.

4. A minister should operate in the spirit of imitative, never waiting to be called on to visit.

5. A minister must always be dressed in appropriate attire. Clergy vestments or business casual attire are rather fitting. Avoid casual clothing.

6. A minister should have a small vial of anointing oil and a Bible in hand.

The following outline may be used during a home visit:

1. Check to ensure that the individual is presentable to receive visitors

2. Upon entrance, greet the ill individual and any other persons present.

3. Engage in meaningful and non-judgmental conversation, asking general questions about the individual's state of being and showing a genuine interest in their life, if possible, assemble those who are present around the place where the sick person is.

4. Say a brief prayer.

5. Its time and setting permit singing a song.

6. Read a passage of scriptures
    (Psalm 46 Psalm 23).

7. Encourage the sick from the passage read.

8. If time and location permits sing another song.

9. Say a prayer for the sick person or persons.

10. Remember to allow the person to say a few words if they desire.

11. Thank the individual for having you there.

12. Finally, don't forget the benediction.

When visiting the sick remember that not all facilities allow a long visit. Besides, the person or persons who are sick needs plenty of rest. Therefore, visitation should be no longer than 20-30 minutes.

CHURCHES DEDICATION

Outdoor Program

Musical interlude

Open hymn prayer

Official Opening of Front Door and Ribbon Cutting

Processional entrance of clergy dignitaries, choir, and congregation.

Indoor Program

Call to worship

Scripture Reading

Prayer

Welcome and Appreciation

Dedication Preliminaries

Church History

Litany of Dedication

Suggested Format

Minister:

Churches are dedicated and consecrated to God for His glory, and honor, for example, King Solomon sought God on how His house should be built by supplication and sacrifices. Due to the providence of God, we have come to this great gathering when the building of our hearts have long desired has become a reality and is to be dedicated to its holy purpose. Let us now unite in prayer, as we thank God for His divine presence, love, goodness, and seek His blessing.

People:

Blessed art Thou, O Lord God, our Father.

Great and mighty things are accomplished through Your power. We bless Your matchless name!

Minister:

We dedicate this Sanctuary to the adoration of God. In the end that Christian worship may be central in the life of this congregation.

People:

God is a spirit and those that worship Him must worship Him in spirit and truth.

Minister:

To the reading of the Holy Scriptures and the witness of the Open Bible, we dedicate this Lectern.

People:

Thy word is a lamp to my feet and a light to my path.

Minister:

Designed for the declaration of the Good News of the Kingdom of God to all who enter this Sanctuary, we dedicate the Pulpit.

People:

Thy Kingdom comes, Thy will be done on earth as it is in Heaven.

Minister

For those who come to receive the Christian ordinance of Baptism as a token of obedience and dedication to life, and who rise to walk in the newness of life, we dedicate this Baptism.

People: we are buried therefore with Him by baptism into death so that as Christ was raised from the dead by the glory of the Father, we too might walk in newness of life.

To Him who said, "I am the light of the world." And for the sake of all to whom He said, "Ye are the light of the World we dedicate these windows.

Minister:

For it is God who said, "Let light shine out of darkness," who has shown in our hears to give the light of the knowledge of the glory of God in the face of Christ

People:

Come to me all who labor and are heavy laden and I will give you rest.

Minister:

To the fragmentary task of World evangelism, we give this house of worship.

People:

You shall be my witness in Jerusalem and all Judea and Samaria to the end of the earth. Amen

Minister:

With great appreciation to all, who by their time, their treasure, their love, and prayers have made this dream a reality. We say thanks and God bless you.

All:

We dedicate this Christian Church.

Minister:

Let us unite in fervent prayer

All:

We consecrate to these, our God, this edifice to be from now on the Holy place of Thy presence with us, and the gateway to eternity. We set it apart from all common use to be Thy Sanctuary, where thy word will be taught and preached. The Laws celebrated, where prayers shall be made unto Thee, and where Thy name shall be mentioned, and Thy Mind and Spirit play upon ours. Let Thy Glory fill this house and dwell in it always. Amen

Dedication of Prayer

Dedication of Anthem from the choir

Addresses from a selected clergyperson, politicians, and public servants

Opening of Doors & Windows

Continuation of Service as Programmed

DEDICATION OF HOME RESIDENCE

Upon entrance of the residence to be blessed:

1. Get there a few minutes before the set time planned.

2. Greet the family politely and ask where the main session will be held.

3. Confer with occupants for the start of the session.

The Ceremony

The Minister should begin with greetings and giving thanks for the occasion, and for beginning invited to do the Ceremony.

Opening Song: My hope is built on nothing less.

Prayer

Scripture reading: Gen 49:22-25; Prov. 28:20; Deut.28:1-14

Minister: Opening Remarks

Other Remarks: Voluntary, or as agreed by congregants

Song: Bless this House

Minister: Blessing of individual areas (optional)

Minister: repeat at the entrance:

O Lord, protect our going out and our coming in let us take pleasure in the warmth of this house with those who visit us, that those who enter may experience your love and peace.

In the living room:

O Lord, grant your blessing to all who share this room that we may be bound collectively in companionship.

In the kitchen:

O Lord, you will satisfy the hungry with excellent things. Grand your blessing on us, as we cook, pray, worship, and work in this kitchen, and make us ever grateful for our bread.

In the dining room:

Holy are you, God of heaven and earth, for you give us food and drinks to preserve our lives and make our hearts merry. Teach us to be thankful for all our mercies, and aware of the desires of others.

In the bedrooms:

Shelter us, O God when we are awake; watch over us as we sleep, that while awake we may keep watch with Christ, and asleep, we may rest in this peace.

In the bathroom:

Holy are you, God of all creation. You formed us in knowledge and love. Refresh us in body and spirit, and keep us in excellent health that we might serve you.

- General Prayer to be offered by all present

- Closing Hymn: Count your blessings

- A final prayer may be offered by the Minister

- The family may offer refreshments, if so, please.

The whole service should last for about an hour. Please do not overstay your visit.

A joyful "goodbye" should be said to the homeowners so they may have time to clean up and retire for the evening.

INSTALLATION OF CHURCH OFFICERS

Officiator:

For the Gospel message to be accomplished in its wholeness, it is significant for laborers to be commissioned for the task. Jesus Christ said the harvest is ripe, but the laborers are few. He instructed us to pray that laborers be sent forth to reap the harvest, after much prayer and as God's line of authority, it pleases us to appoint {name} to the office of {officer}.

Officiator: At this time, I would like to invite {name} to approach the pulpit for consecration.

Congregational Song: Recommended Jesus Use Me

Covenant of Dedication

Led by officiator, usually a pastor/bishop or another clergyperson

Officiator:

We are gathered here in the name of the Lord, Jesus, and in His holy presence to consecrate {name}, who has answered the call to become {officer} in the name of Jesus Christ. As this is a solemn act that involves mutual obligations, I call upon you to unite the covenant of dedication.

Officiator:

Are you willing to work as a/an {officer} agreeable to your declaration of accepting His call?

Candidate:

Yes, I am willing

Officiator:

Do you willfully believe and proclaim that in taking upon you this charge, you are influenced by a genuine wish to promote (and preach-optional depending on the office) the Gospel of the Kingdom, to the glory of God and for the good of the church?

Officiator:

Do you solemnly promise that, by the help of the grace of God, you will live a sacred and sanctified life with the Lord, while endeavoring to faithfully discharge all the duties of the said office, and will be careful to maintain a department in all respect becoming a servant of the Gospel of Christ in affirming your ordination vows?

Candidate:

Yes, I do

Officiator:

Do you accept your responsibility to serve {name of the assemble}, as well as the extended and international Body of Christ, in the office to which you have been chosen? Do you reaffirm your loyalty to this assembly? Will you commit yourself to assist in keeping the reputation above reproach in the city, nation, and the world? Are you willing to accept your pastor as the spiritual and business leader of {GLC} under the preview of the Lord Jesus Christ, the Bishop, and Shepherd of the Church? Are you willing to protect your role as a helper and do your best to work with the pastor and the members of the ecclesiastical body as they are led by the Lord?

Candidate:

Yes, I am willing and will do what is required of me by the word of God and the leadership of the assembly.

Officiator:

Along with the mission and vision statement and the existing rules and covenants that govern {GLC}, do you solemnly swear to uphold and promote the fundamental doctrines of the Apostolic faith, established by Jesus Christ himself which include the call to genuine repentance of humanity water baptism in the name of Jesus Christ the baptism of the Holy Ghost with the mandatory and initial evidence of speaking in tongues, the call unto holiness in daily living.

Candidate:

I will, by the grace of God,

Recommended Hymn: A charge to Keep I Have

Prayer of Consecration

Officiator, along with the Broad of Directors and other officers will proceed to anoint candidate(s) with oil and lay hands as the officiators prayers.

Ministerial Charge

II Timothy 4:1-5- to be read

Officiator:

In the name of the Lord, Jesus Christ, who is the Supreme Head of the Church, I now present {name}, to the congregation!

Officiator:

{Name}, we commit you into the able hands of Almighty God to perform the work of a/ an {office}. As you carry out the responsibility of this office, I implore you to walk worthy of this vocation, you will be rewarded with a crown of life that will never fade. May, the goodness mercy, and abundant blessings of the Lord ever be with you as you embark and participate in the continuation of the earth of our Lord until He comes.

Song: All the way My Savior Leads Me

EVANGELISM

Why do we evangelize?

We believe the purpose of evangelism is to promote the gospel to a lost and dying world, so they know that Jesus is Lord. Jesus gave the great commission to His disciples to go into all the earth and preach the gospel. Matthew 28:19-20 says, "Go ye therefore and teach all nations, baptizing them in the name of the Father and of the Son and the Holy Ghost: Teaching them to observe all things whatsoever I commanded you: and, lo I am with you always, even unto to the end of the world" Through spreading the good news lives are changed and souls are save for the kingdom of God. We evangelize through witnessing, distribution of tracks in our local community, public outreach, and preaching locally, and internationally. Other methods are facilitated in nursing homes, hospitals, and home settings. Witnessing is necessary for the Gospel of Jesus Christ to be spread. The Bible noted in Acts 8 :1 "But ye shall receive power after the Holy Ghost has come upon you: and ye shall be witness onto me both in Jerusalem and in all Judea, and Samaria and unto the uttermost part of the earth".

Door–to–Door Approach

This ministry is extremely effective because one can witness one on one with an individual in their community who needs Christ. Besides, a title's personal touch never hurts as one hand out the appropriate literature.

- It's good, to begin with, a smile, and please wear your mask.

- Please bring appropriate literature to hand out in the community.

The following are good ways to approach this area of ministry.

Approach # 1

- Good afternoon, how are you today?

- My name is{name}.

- I am from {GLC} located at{684 Springfield Avenue Newark N, J}.

- Today we are in the neighborhood to invite children to our Sunday school.

The obvious question most of the time is, what kind of religious group you are?

1. We are an Apostolic or Pentecostal church.

2. Have you ever been to an Apostolic or Pentecostal church before?

3. If you have not we would love to invite you to visit us.

Conversations are tailored from this point and you can get a commission.

Approach # 2

- Tailor your approach and response to what the person presents;

- Also to the nature of your church and your community-related programs (e.g .food-bank academic etc.) you are offering.

CHURCH PLANTING

Why do we do church planting?

Acts 13-14; 16; 20 Thess 1:2-10 Titus 1:5

As believers, we follow the example given in the Holy Bible and establish churches throughout the nations, in essence, to spread the gospel of our Lord Jesus Christ to lost souls.

We wholly follow the illustration of the Apostle Paul One of the first pioneers of church planting. A Pharisee who was converted by God on the road to Damascus. Once known as Saul of Tarsus, he persecuted the Jews for believing in Jesus Christ. Nevertheless, when he was transformed by the power of the Holy Ghost, he took the gospel of Jesus Christ all over the world to places such as Asia Minor. His missionary movements empowered other Christians such as Titus, Timothy, and Philemon. When a new church extension is established, it should be understood that the parent Pastor will be overseeing the new church extension until such time that he/she deems fit to appoint a resident pastor. In the interim, the pastor will appoint a minister to assist him/her at the new location. A reasonable compensation plan should be worked out to assist the entirety of the ministry.

MINISTERIAL CODE OF ETHICS

A code of ethics is a set of principles for ministerial behavior prescribed in the Holy Bible.

As a servant of the Lord why must we live by a Code of Ethics, and what is a Code of Ethics? Below is a list of the characteristics that a candidate must possess according to the Word of God to be an ordained minister.

1. Must be saved according to the Apostolic creed-baptized in the name of Jesus Christ, filled with the Holy Ghost, and living a holy life.

2. Must have genuine love, care, and compassion for the souls of mankind.

3. Must be passionate about soul—winning.

4. Must be apt to learn and a student of the Bible.

5. Must have a good prayer and fasting life.

6. Demonstrate compassion for the poor and concern for the broken heart, must have a forgiving spirit.

7. Must seek peace and pursue it.

8. Must lead by example.

9. Must be a person that cares and prioritizes ministry work.

10. Must be a person that respects time (an integral part of leadership).

11. Must be a person who is true to his word.

12. Must be trustworthy; keep things in confidence, etc.

The minister as an individual

1. A minister must always be cognizant of the holy vocation to which he/she is called.

2. A minister must make every effort to live according to the word of God and cultivate Christ-like characteristics.

3. A minister should maintain an active life of prayer, fasting, and Bible study to foster his/her relationship with God. This enables them to carry out, their ecclesiastical duties with power,

4. A minister must be a leader in his/her home, along with his/her spouse, providing ample and essential discipline, and emotional support. 1 Time 3:5

5. A minister must always manage his/her financial and business transactions honestly.

6. A minister must have high moral standards in his/her public and private appearance, conduct, and speech.

The Apostolic Clergy person in the American Context

1. A minister should seek to reflect, improve and support his/her home church and organization as well as the unity initiatives of the Canadian Apostolic Ministries, and aim to maintain their good reputation at all times.

2. A minister should make every effort to attend pastoral meetings.

3. A minister should honor the office of the region and it's national leadership.

General Covenants of the Ministry for all Clergypersons

Responsibility to American Apostolic Ministries

1. I will love, support, and cooperate with the American Apostolic Ministries and the faith community of which I am a part.

2. I will commit myself to working with the American Apostolic Ministries in its efforts to expand and extend the Kingdom of God.

Responsibility to Self

1. I will maintain my physical and emotional health by taking proper care of my body, having good eating habits, and exercising.

2. I take care of my depositional life by a consistent time of Scriptures reading, meditation prayer, and fasting.

3. I will continue to grow intellectually through reading comprehensive, personal study, and attending development conferences.

4. I will balance personal obligations, church duties, and family responsibilities by managing my time right.

5. Unless otherwise permitted I will avoid interfering in the affairs of another assembly.

6. Within my surrounding community I will endeavor to participate in activities with the view of meeting the social needs of people and ultimately, spreading the Gospel of Jesus Christ

7. In my Christian living and finances, I will be honest.

8. In attitude and action toward all persons regardless of race, social class, religious beliefs, or position of influence within the church and the community I will seek to be Christ-like.

9. I will be true in speech, never plagiarizing another's work, exaggerating facts, misusing personal experiences, or communicating gossip.

Responsibility to the Family

1. I will seek to endeavor to maintain a proper balance between my responsibility to my family, which is primary, and my responsibilities within the ministry as a minister.

2. I will be fair to every member of my family, giving ample time, love, and consideration to each. I will seek to be a servant-minister of the church by following the example of the Lord Jesus Christ.

3. I will regard my children as a gift from God and seek to meet their individual needs without imposing undue expectations upon them.

Responsibility to the Local Assembly

1. I will seek to be a servant-minister of the church by following the example of Christ in faith, love, wisdom, courage, and integrity.

2. Through evangelistic responsibility, I will seek to lead persons to salvation and church membership without manipulating converts, proselytizing members of other churches, or demeaning other religious faiths.

3. Through visitation and counseling practices, I will never be alone with a person of the opposite sex unless another church member is present nearby.

4. When leaving a parishioner, I will try to strengthen the house of worship through proper timing, verbal/written affirmation, and an appropriate closure of my ministry.

5. I will seek to protect my assembly from potential harm, whether spiritual or emotional, by refraining from giving ministry privileges, whether oral or written, to any questionable person.

Responsibility to Contemporaries

1. I will endeavor to tell all ministers, particularly those with whom I serve in my assemble, as partners in the work of God, in respect of their ministry and cooperating with it.

2. I will seek to serve my minister contemporaries and their families with counsel, support, receive, and personal assistance.

3. I will decline to treat any minister as a rivalry to gain a church, an honor, or attain statistical success.

4. I will abstain from speaking judgmentally about the person or work of any other minister, particularly my forerunner or successor.

5. I will improve the ministry of my heir by not impeding in any way the church I previously served.

6. I will treat with admiration, and politeness, any predecessor who comes back to my church field

7. I will revisit a former church for specialized services, such as weddings and funerals in consolation with the resident pastor.

8. I will be caring and respectful of all retired ministers and, upon my retirement, I will support and be devoted to my pastor.

9. I will be sincere and kind in my reference of other ministers to church positions or other inquiries.

10. If cognizant of any serious accusation of misconduct by a minister, I will endeavor to engage the "Abuse Policy and Procedure" of the Gospel Light Ministries.

Responsibility to the Community

1. I will consider my key accountability to be pastor of my congregation and will never neglect official duties to serve the public

2. I will take reasonable responsibilities for public services, knowing that the preacher has a public ministry.

3. I will support public morality in the community through responsible prophetic witness and social action.

4. I will follow the rules of the government unless they require my defiance of the commandments of God.

Pastors

1. In my managerial and pastoral obligations, I will be fair to all members.

2. I will devotedly discharge my time and energies as pastor through appropriate work habits and reasonable schedules.

3. I will give adequate time to prayer and preparation in my preaching responsibility so my presentation will be biblically sound, theologically correct, and communicated.

4. I will maintain strict confidentiality, in pictorial counseling, except in cases in which disclosure is necessary to prevent harm to the person and/or is required by law.

5. I will establish policies based on ministry opportunities, time, and theology, for non-members; I will not charge church members for weddings or funerals.

6. I will perform my duties in the spirit of meekness; I will embrace my office in the Lord's Church as holy.

7. I recognize my responsibility as a spiritual guide to God's sheep, the saints of the parishioners, and members of my nearby community.

8. I will try to be enthusiastically involved in the harvest of souls on local national and international levels.

Elders, Ministers, Evangelists, Missionaries, & Deacons

1. To the senior pastor, I will be supportive and loyal.

2. I will forever be responsible to the senior pastor and all other church officers over me.

3. I will be supportive of and loyal to my fellow staff minister, never criticizing them or undermining their ministry.

4. I will acknowledge my position and duty to church staff and will not feel endangered or in opposition with any other minister of the church.

5. In my special area of ministry, I will maintain good relationships with other ministers.

6. I will be impartial and fair in my administrative duties.

7. I will gladly discharge my time and efforts as a representative of the assembly through proper work ethics and reasonable schedules.

8. In my preaching responsibilities, I will give ample time to study and pray so my presentation will be biblically sound, theologically correct, and communicated

Counselors

1. I will have a pastor/counselor to who I can turn for counseling and advice.

2. I will be attentive to my requirements and vulnerabilities, never seeking to meet my personal needs through my counselees.

3. I will know the power I hold over counselees and never take advantage of their weakness through exploitation or manipulation

4. I will never become sexually or passionately mixed up with a customer or engage in any form of erotic or loving contact.

5. Irrespective of their morals, beliefs, attitudes, or actions, I will show unconditional acceptance and love towards all counselees.

6. I will refer a client to another professional who can provide appropriate therapy if I am unable to benefit him or her.

7. I will keep private all matters discussed in a counseling setting unless the information is hazardous for the customer or another person or by law must be disclosed.

8. I will offer my support and services to fellow clerics and their families whenever needed.

9. I will support and contribute to the ministry of my church through personal counseling lectures, workshops, group therapy, and seminars.

10. I will seek to upkeep the policies and beliefs of my church without unduly imposing them on any counselee.

The Appearance of the Minister (Officer) (this should reflect both female and male ministers)

As a minister of Christ, your appearance is important. Endeavor for a fresh, neat, clean-cut, such as close shave, well-groomed, clean face, hands, and polished shoes. As well as pressed suits, tie for men, polished shoes, appropriate dress, skirt, and blouse for women.

Appropriate oral and body hygiene is the most important when appearing before parishioners and interacting with people. Your hygiene must be at the highest standard at all times.

It is a saying that he or she who becomes careless in their appearance has also become thoughtless in studying the word and preparing for sermons as well as personal matters.

Although one's clothing does not make a man, yet it brings about great influence on both save and unsaved people.

Do avoid flashy clothes, rings, jewelry, and dress modesty. You are a judge at times based on your reappearance, has the minister always remembered to dress appropriately, when appearing before an audience formal or semi-formal.

Don't carry large items in your pocket when standing before an audience because they may bulge.

When preaching it is suggested you wear a light robe.

CHRISTIAN STEWARDSHIP

Malachi 3:8, 9 Genesis 14: 18-23 Gen. 1:26-28 Genesis 14:20

When God entrusts Christians with money and property, then we must give back a tenth of our earnings to God as instructed in the Holy Scriptures.

The principle of tithing is depicted throughout the Bible all in Genesis. Christian stewardship is living according to the commandments of God's word and doing what it says, for example, God requires us to give a tenth of our salary and any increase to His church to further His Kingdom. We recognize that all our possessions belong to God for this reason we wholeheartedly follow His commandments. In Sacred Scriptures, we find many examples of stewardship like Abraham having to pay a tenth of his wages to Melchizedek a form of Christ. **Genesis 14:20** states, "And blessed be the most high God, who has delivered your enemies into thy hand, he gave him a tenth of all." The idea of stewardship originates from the beginning of time when God gave dominion of the earth to Adam and Eve and their children (**Gen. 1:26-28**). If we obey God's law and give Him what he asked for He will bless us abundantly and if not we are a curse as the Holy Scriptures state.

What is tithing?

The tithe is the tenth part (10%) of all things dedicated to sacred use.

What is Christian Stewardship?

God asked the prophet Malachi a question regarding Christian Stewardship in the Bible, "Will a man rob God? Yet ye have robbed me. But ye say wherein have we robbed thee? In tithes and offerings. Ye are cursed with a curse: for ye have robbed me, even this whole nation. Bring ye all the tithes into the storehouse, that there may be meat in mine house, and prove me now herewith, saith the Lord of hosts, if I will not open you the windows of heaven, and pour you out a blessing, that there shall not be room enough to receive it" **(Malachi 3:8- 9).**

History of tithing

- Tithed exists before the Law

- Abraham paid tithed (Genesis 14:20)

- Malachi 3:8,9

- Tithed exists under the law

- Israel as a nation tithed (Leviticus 2:7 30-33, Numbers 18: 20-32).

- Tithing occurred under grace

- Jesus confirm tithing in Matthew

- Paul taught tithing in the New Testament epistles:
  1 Corinthian 9:7-14, Paul was making a direct comparison to the priesthood.

  In Galatians 6.6 the Amplified Bible explains to us the word "communicate" to mean ministerial support " Let him who receives instruction in the Word (of God) share all good thing with his teacher—contributing to his support."

1. Tithing was not created under the law but before it.

(Hebrews 7:1-21) Verse 8 tells us "…Here men…receive tithes…

Is it necessary for believers to tithe today?

Yes. God admonishes us to tithe (Leviticus 27:30; Proverbs 3:9-10).

If a person does not tithe and presents offerings to God, he is robbing God (Malachi 3:8-10).

The tithe is not for us to keep, it is God's possession. We are just giving God what belongs to Him. However, if a person only tithes, and does not gives an offering he/she is not giving anything to God at all.

"Will a man rob God? Yet ye have robbed me. But ye say, wherein have we robbed thee? In tithes and offerings. ye are curse with a curse; for ye have robbed me even this whole nation. Bring ye all the tithes into the storehouse, that they are meat in my house, and prove me now herewith, said the Lord of host, if I will not open up the windows of heaven, and pour you out a blessing, that there shall not be room enough to receive it. And I will rebuke the devourer for your sakes, and he shall not destroy the fruits of your ground; said the Lord of host. And all nations shall call you blessed: for ye shall be a delight to the land, said the Lord of host. (Malachi 3:8-12).

Where is the tithe to be given?

To the storehouse of God (Malachi 3:8-12).

- The storehouse is where one gets spiritual sustenance.

- The storehouse to Israel was the tabernacle

- The local church is the storehouse for the New Testaments believer today.

Is the offering the same as the tithe?

No, it is a gift to God above our regular tithe.

One can give beyond what is asked for. One gives at their discretion.

There is a difference made between the two in the word of God (Malachi 3:8-12).

In what different ways does the scripture tells us to give?

- Tithes: the portion given to God in our local storehouse (assembly).

- Offering: that which is given to support programs, and other ministries of the church, locally or internationally. For example Missions programs, building funds (in our community or abroad) Evangelism, or outreach programs.

- Alm: as well as a gift to a person, confidentially (Matthew 6:1-4).

What kind of attitudes are to be had in the hearts of those who give unto God?

- Give "freely" (11 Corinthians 8:3-12)

- Give "cheerfully" (11 Corinthians 9:7)

- Give "thankfully" (11 Corinthians 9:11-12)

- Give "lovely" (11 Corinthians 8:24)

- Give with "pure heart" (Matthew 6:24)

SECTION 3: CHURCH POLICIES & PROCEDURES

What are Church Policies & Procedures?

Church policies are essential for us as Christians to follow because they guide us in the right direction. They help to govern and discipline us. God is a God of order and order must be in His house and our lives for Christians to make it to eternity.?

GLC SEXUAL HARASSMENT POLICY STATEMENT AND PROCEDURE

The following policy statement is designed to help members of Gospel Light Ministries **(GLC) become** aware of behavior that is sexual harassment and to outline the procedure GLC will use to deal with sexual harassment in a way that protects complainants, witnesses, and respondents.

No members of GLC must engage in sexual harassment they have a moral responsibility to assist in creating a climate at each associated church so that sexual harassment does not happen. GLC has no tolerance for such behavior of its leadership, members, volunteers, and supporters.

Definitions:

The following definition is to help make clear the reading of policy:

Associated church: Used to denote a church in membership with GLC whether reporting directly to or indirectly working with.

Complainant: the person against whom the alleged sexual harassment incident was committed.

Credibility Committee: will consist of trained individuals skilled in investigating professionally and confidentially.

Investigator; A trained and qualified person assigned by GLC to secure information on cases presented for investigation.

Leader: Will be used to demote one in authority as follows: a bishop; overseer; pastor; evangelist; teacher; minister; deacon; missionary; president; or vice –president; chief executive officer; director; chairperson; administrator; coordinator; facilitator; supervisor; or board member.

Member: This Will be used to denote a brother or sister a volunteer or an employee over 16 years old.

Respondent: The individual whom the allegations of sexual harassment are made.

What is Sexual Harassment?

Sexual Harassment includes unwelcome sexual advances, requests for sexual favors, and other verbal or physical conduct of a sexual nature that tends to create a hostile, intimidating, or offensive fellowship and work environment.

For purposes of this policy, Sexual harassment includes but is not limited to the following.

- Unwelcome sexual advances

- Sexual remarks sexual innuendos and comments

- Insulting sounds or suggestive obscene

- Displaying cartoons or posters of a sexual nature; writing sexual suggestions letters, blogs, or notes.

- Eyeballing someone suggestively.

- Telling a woman she is not suited for a particular position.

- Asking for a date consistently after being refused.

- Commenting on someone's sexual unattractiveness or attractiveness

- Touching a person in a sexual way

- Questions and discussion about someone's sexual life.

- Actual denial of a position-related benefit for refusal to comply with a sexual request per

- Implied or expressed threat of reprisal for refusal to comply with a sexual request.

- Patting, pinching, or brushing up against another's body in a sexually suggestive manner

- All of the above applies to cyberspace as well

Hence sexual harassment can be verbal, physical, visual, or written. When committed by those in a leadership positions that constitute sexual harassment, as well as members who indulge in these behaviors, are subject to disciplinary actions. GLC prohibits these and all other forms of sexual behavior.

Casualty of Sexual Harassment

List cost of this behavior on the human body.

Bequest for GLC Ministry Involvement in Harassment Allegations

GLC's participation and invoking of the Policy will be dependent on a request from an Assembly (Church)

Via:

- The Church Board

- The Government

- The Pastor or bishop

- Its Organization
  member of a Congregation

- The Victim, and;

- Only with the consent of the Board or Leadership of the organization and or the Local Assembly from which the allegation came.

Electronic Publication

If there is a case where a serious accusation is made and could become civic knowledge, and this individual's contact is on the GLC website or church website, it will be removed immediately until there is appropriate dispute resolution.

Complaints Involving Lay Membership

Wherever an accusation involves a Pastor or Bishop and they are removed from their leadership role, deliberation will be given for the well-being of the membership.

In consultation with the Official Board of the Assembly, GLC will provide for the following:

- Well-timed information to the Official Board

- Proper, timed information to the church

- If needed, provided additional grief therapy

- At the end of the leader's tenure, temporary or permanent, GLC will provide an appropriate leader as a temporary or permanent replacement, from the immediate body of Christ. If a fitting applicant is not available, the GLC will act as a go-between with respective associates or organizations to pursue proper steps to provide an external candidate.

- GLC will make recommendations outlining the level of participation of the accused.

- All through and after the procedure, GLC may connect in a dialogue concerning pecuniary obligations towards the accused.

- GLC will work with the offender, to understand any potential healing and restoration.

- If a re-installation of the leader is possible through the reconciliation process, this will be followed through with utmost care and communication.

Procedure

1. 0 General Reporting & Investigation

1.1 Members who have complaints of sexual harassment relating to the leader's co-members volunteers, clients, volunteers' vendors, workers, or workers, are encouraged to report such behavior to the Gospel Light Ministries (GLM) report the abuse line. The report abuse contact information is available on the GLM website:gospellight684@yahoo.com.gospellight2@yahoo.com. gospel.light.admin@gmail.com. Saints are advised to bring their concerns to be investigated within (14) of the alleged incidents(s).

1.2 A suitable person or group of individuals will be assigned to investigate the complaints. The inspector will investigate all complaints as proceedings will be expositional maintained.

The grievance investigation will begin thirty (30) days or less after the complaint is received.

1.3 The investigator will determine when, where and with whom a meeting will take place to talk about the result of the complaint.

1.4 The examiner must be in attendance at all meetings between the complainant and respondent private documentation of each meeting is encouraged.

1.5 Any saint who is found to have partaken in sexual harassment will be subject to disciplinary action, which may include verbal or written reprimand, demotion, membership termination, transfer, or dismissal.

2.0 Retaliation

There will be no retaliation against a member for reporting sexual harassment or assisting in the investigation of a grievance. Any revenge against such person of a complaint or any retaliation against the individual is subject to disciplinary action, as well as verbal or written reprimands

3.0 False Complaints

If after investigation any complaint of sexual harassment, is revealed that the complaint is not true or that person has given false information regarding the complaint; that individual may be subject to disciplinary action. Suitable actions will be taken to make sure that the character of the respondent is not defamed.

Investigation of an Informal Complaint

GLM's key priority will be to attempt to determine the complaint through a mutual agreement between the complainant and the respondent.

4.1 Any member can talk about an informal complaint with an Investigator.

4-2 If the complainant who discusses an informal complaint is not willing to be identified to the respondent, the Investigation will make a confidential record of the situation and will offer guidance regarding the various ways to resolve the issue. This documentation will be held in confidence.

4.3 For example, if any member bringing a complaint is prepared to be identified to the respondent and wishes to attempt an informal resolution of the problem, the circumstances (signed by the complainant) and undertake appropriate discussions with the parties involved.

4.4 when an individual or member reports incidents is willing or sexual harassment that has occurred in a public context (for instance, offensive sexual remarks in an office setting) or when the investigator receives repeated complaints from different members that an individual has engaged in sexual harassment, the respondent will be informed without revealing the identity of the complainants

5.0 Investigation of a Formal Complaint

5.1 For example, if a member desires to follow the matter through an official resolution, a written complaint must be submitted describing the detail of the so-called harassment, including dates, times, places, names(s) of the person(s) involved, and names of any witness.

5.2 The complaint must be addressed to the investigator.

5.3 The names or other identifying information regarding witnesses for either party involved in the complaint will not be made known to the respondent.

5.4 Once the investigator receives a copy of the written complaint, he will immediately forward a letter stating the complaint, along with a copy of GLM's Harassment Policy

Statement by mail, courier, or electronic mail, to the respondent and request a meeting within three days, of receipt of the formal complaint notification.

5.5 The researcher will be limited to what is essential to resolve the complaint to suggest at the discretion of the investigator. If it is needed for the investigator to speak to any persons other than those involved in the complaint. He will do so only after informing the complainants and respondents.

5.6 The researcher will examine all complaints of sexual Harassment expeditiously and efficiently. To the point possible, the investigation will be complete within thirty (30) days from the time and formal investigation is initiated.

5.7 For an instant, if the investigation does not produce an answer within the time permitted, the complainant will be told as soon as possible.

5.8 The researcher will keep the confidentiality of the information provided to them concerning the complaints and investigation process. The only other person of GLM who will be knowledgeable regarding the investigation is the President of GLM.

5.9 The referrals for therapists and medical personnel for all persons concerned in an investigation will be made accessible upon request.

6.0 Resolution

After the conclusion of an investigation, the researcher will construct one of the following determinations:

6.1 Complaint Sustain: A ruling of Sexual Harassment has been made and suggestions for corrective action will be identified.

6.2 Complaint Not Sustain: A ruling of no sexual Harassment has been made. The complaint will be obligated to make an admission of guilt (verbally if the complaint was informal or written if the complaint was formal).

6.3 Insufficient Information: inadequate information exists on which to decide. The researcher will reinvestigate based on new proof regarding the original complaint.

7.0 Recommended Corrective Action

The reason for any recommended corrective action is to determine a complaint, correct or remedy the injury, if any, to the complainant, and to stop further harassment.

7.1 Recommended action may include a private or public apology, written or oral reprimand of the respondent, relief from specific duties, suspension, transfer, membership termination, or dismissal of the individual who engaged in sexual harassment. In addition, mandatory counseling helps a person to further address the roof of behavior.

7.2 Punitive action that may engage in a financial cost and/or treatment for mental/medical services.

7.3 Following any determination or recommendation for corrective action, the researcher will present written documents with findings of information and basis and recommendation to the Credibility Committee of GLM.

7.4 The Credibility Committee will communicate with the complainant and take action regarding investigative findings and suggestion for corrective action.

7.5 As a result, if complaints are not pleased with the attempts to decide the sexual harassment, they may search for resolution through other sources, like the Human Rights Commission.

Policy Limitation

This policy will not be called upon where the event involves a minor, as the law of the land will l take precedence.

Policy Review

This policy will be reviewed occasionally by the GLM Sexual Harassment Policy committee.

MINISTERIAL CERTIFICATE/ CREDENTIAL

Apostolic Church

684 Springfield Avenue

Newark, New Jersey 07103

Ministerial Certificate

This is to certify that line of the line has been called by the Holy Ghost as a line and is working in conjunction with the Apostolic Church. The above name line is endowed with all rights and privileges as a(a) line according to God's Holy Word.

President: line seal is here

Secretary: line

Issued: line

Valid with a current Fellowships Card.

LETTER OF INVITATION TO SERVICE

Fordperice Apostolic

Florida

Phone (862) 763-9078

Fax (862) 556-9870

[Date of composition]

Dear Pastor & Saints

Please accept holy and sincere greetings in the mighty name of Jesus Christ!

It is with great pleasure that we extend this invitation to you and your congregation to attend our {Women's Conference}, scheduled for {4/18/2018}. Our theme is {theme}, founded upon[scripture text]. We are happy to have [name(s) of speaker] as our keynote speaker(s).

We expect a glorious time of powerful praise, and soul-winning in the presence of the Lord and we look forward to having you fellowship with us. May the good Lord bless you richly.

Working for the Kingdom of Almighty God,

Bishop, Stuart Smith

Overseer

LETTER OF INVITATION & CONFIRMATION FOR GUEST SPEAKER

Apostolic Church of God

Patterson, New Jersey

Phone: (973) 862-9087

Date of composition

[Full name of recipient]

Address

Dear [recipient]

Please accept holy and sincere greetings in the mighty name of Jesus!

Thanks for accepting our invitation to be our guest speaker at our **[name of event]** to be held **[date]**. We are thrilled about the upcoming meeting and are honored that God has so positioned you to partake with us in the ministry of the word.

The theme of the meeting is**[theme & scripture text]**. You are scheduled to minister on **[clearly state date(s) & time (s) when guest will speak]**.

We look forward to fellowshipping with you.

Until then, may the good Lord bless you richly.

In His Service,

Sharon Taylor

Secretary

MINISTERIAL APPRECIATION LETTER

Mount Zion Apostolic church

1357 Liverpool Avenue

Ontario, Canada 09876

[Date of composition]

Full name of the recipient

Address

It is with great pleasure that I greet you in the holy and sincere name of Jesus Christ! In Him, we live, love, joy, breath, and have our being.

On behalf of the {name of church} family, I would like to thank you for joining us for our [name of event and theme]. Your ministry has been a blessing to our assembly. Each word was refreshing, awesome, and God-inspired.

It is our wish that God will continually be the joy of your life, and lead you into complete victory. Be all God has called you to be and in doing so, you will bring honor to His glorious name!

In appreciation to the Lord,

Bishop Stuart Smith

Overseer

CONTACT INFORMATION

Gospel Apostolic Ministries

Mailing Address:

684 Springfield Avenue

Newark, New Jersey

07103

973-372-7562

http://www.gospellight684.org

Gospellight684@yahoo.com

NOTES

Bishop Stuart Smith

Bishop Stuart Smith is the founder of Gospel Light Church. Through divine direction and vision, the Gospel Light Church of God in Christ Jesus, (Apostolic) Inc. was established in 1977. For the first few months services were held in Bishop Smith's home; however, with God's unmerited favor and the faithful members, the church relocated to a small storefront property at 721 Springfield Avenue where the first service was held in September of 1977.

Later Bishop Smith purchased 684 Springfield Avenue. Since the purchase of 684 Springfield Avenue, God has blessed Bishop Smith to purchase 688-692 Springfield Avenue. In 1992 Gospel Light Christian Academy was established. Bishop Smith has been awarded for his efforts in the community and worldwide, he was presented with an achievement certificate from both the Mayor of Newark and the governor of New Jersey.

song

Change me, Lord

Change me, Lord

Touch me, Lord

Change me, Lord

I want to be touched by you.

Change me, Lord

Touch me, Lord

I want to be touched by you.

Touch me, Lord

I want to be changed by you.

I want to be used by you.

I AM AN EAGLE

12/6/2022
7:00 P.M.

God said I shall rise again.
The righteous man falls 7 times but
he shall rise again.
Like an eagle, I shall rise again.
After every storm, I shall rise again.
Even when setbacks come, God said I shall rise again.
Like an eagle soaring above all obstacles, hindrances, and distractions.
Not stopping until I reach my destination.
I shall rise again.
I shall rise again.
God said I shall rise again.
I shall rise again
Yes, I will rise again in JESUS' name.
Like an eagle soaring without end, I shall rise again over all my enemies.
God said I shall rise again.
Yes, I shall rise again.

FEAR NOT I AM WITH YOU!

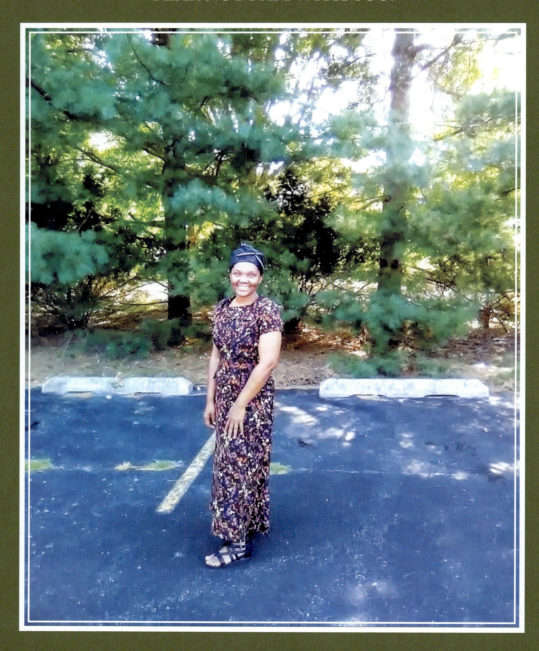

GOD IS ABLE TO DO WHAT HE SAID HE WOULD DO!

DON'T GIVE UP ON GOD!

Printed in the United States
by Baker & Taylor Publisher Services